DATE DUE

Material Detectives: Wood
Let's Look at a Baseball Bat

Angela Royston

Heinemann Library
Chicago, Illinois

Customer Service   888-454-2279

Visit our website at www.heinemannlibrary.com

Printed and bound in China by South China Printing Company Limited
Photo research by Erica Newbery

10 09 08 07 06
10 9 8 7 6 5 4 3 2 1

Library of Congress Cataloging-in-Publication Data
Royston, Angela.
   Wood : let's look at a baseball bat / Angela Royston.
       p. cm. -- (Material detectives)
   Includes index.
   ISBN 1-4034-7672-1 (library binding-hardcover) -- ISBN 1-4034-7681-0 (pbk.)
   1. Wood--Juvenile literature. 2. Baseball bats--Juvenile literature. I. Title: Let's look at a baseball bat. II. Title. III. Series.
   TA419.R676 2005
   620.1'2--dc22

                                                              2005004706

Acknowledgments
The author and publishers are grateful to the following for permission to reproduce copyright material:
Alamy/Banana Stock p. 6; Banana Stock/Alamy p. 12; Brand X Pictures/Alamy pp. **10**, **16**; Harcourt Education p. **5**; Ron Chapple/Alamy p. **4**; Tudor Photography/Harcourt Education Ltd pp. backcover (stone and ball), **7**, **8**, **9**, **11**, **13**, **14**, **15**, **17**, **18**, **19**, **20**, **21**, **22**, **23** (all), **24**.

Cover photograph of baseball bats reproduced with permission of Jim Cornfield/Corbis.

Every effort has been made to contact copyright holders of any material reproduced in this book. Any omissions will be rectified in subsequent printings if notice is given to the publisher.

Many thanks to the teachers, library media specialists, reading instructors, and educational consultants who have helped develop the Read and Learn/Lee y aprende brand.

Some words are shown in bold, **like this**. They are explained in the glossary on page 23.

Contents

What is a Baseball Bat? 4

What Does a Bat Look Like? 6

Is a Bat Heavy or Light? 10

Is a Bat Rough or Smooth? 14

Is a Bat Hard or Soft? 16

Is a Bat Bendy or Rigid? 18

Do Baseball Bats Rot? 20

Quiz 22

Glossary 23

Index 24

What is a Baseball Bat?

A bat is used to play a game.

The pitcher throws the ball.

The batter tries to hit the ball with the bat.

What Does a Bat Look Like?

This bat is long and rounded.

It is easy to hold.

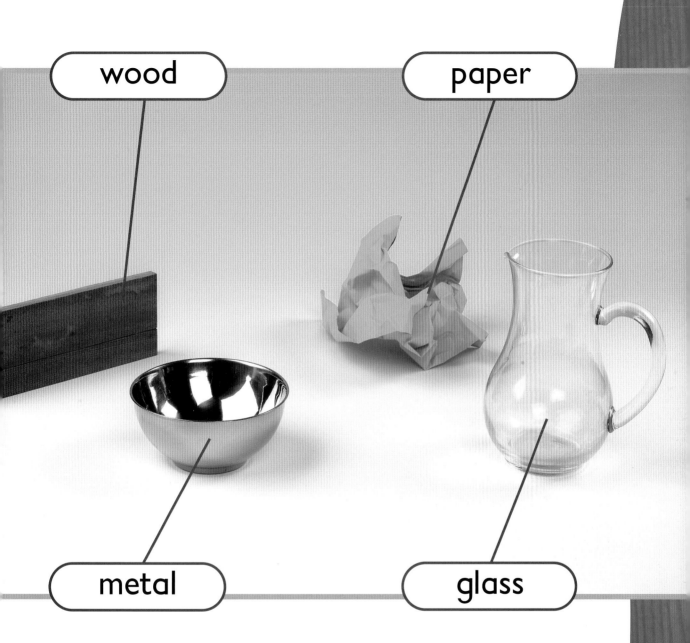

wood

paper

metal

glass

What **material** is the bat made of?

A bat is made of wood.

Can you see the swirly patterns in this wood?

Wood can be **carved** into many different shapes.

These things are made of wood, too.

Is a Bat Heavy or Light?

A wooden bat is quite heavy.

It can hit a ball hard.

Is a wooden bat heavier or lighter than a plastic bat?

Wood is heavier than plastic.

You use two hands to swing a wooden bat.

Wood is lighter than rock.

A bat made of rock would be too heavy to pick up.

Is a Bat Rough or Smooth?

Some wood is **rough**.

Rough wood can give you splinters, so be careful!

A wooden bat is rubbed and polished to make the wood smooth.

Is a Bat Hard or Soft?

A bat is hard.

The ball bounces off the hard surface of the bat.

A ball does not bounce off a pillow.

This is because the pillow is soft.

Is a Bat Bendy or Rigid?

Can you bend a bat?

No, a bat is strong and **rigid**.

A bat is more rigid than a **hose**.

A hose is bendy.

Do Bats Rot?

Some wood rots if it gets wet.

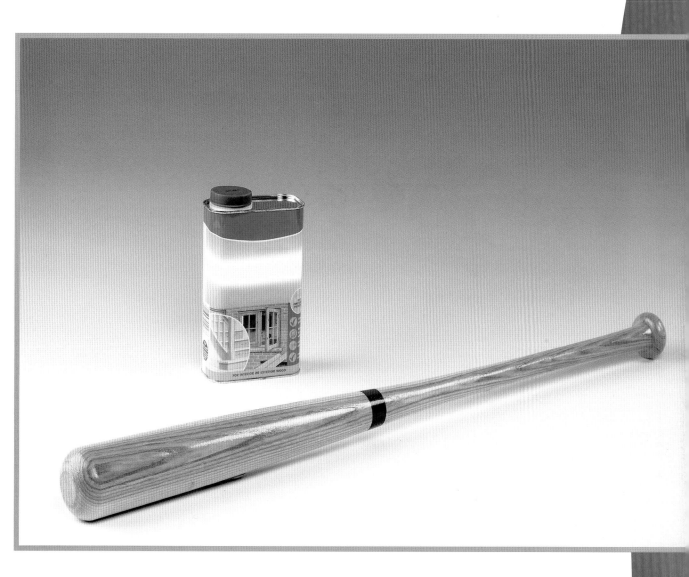

A baseball bat does not rot.

The wood has been soaked in special **chemical preservative**.

Quiz

Which of these things are hard like a bat?

Which of them are soft?

Look for the answers on page 24.

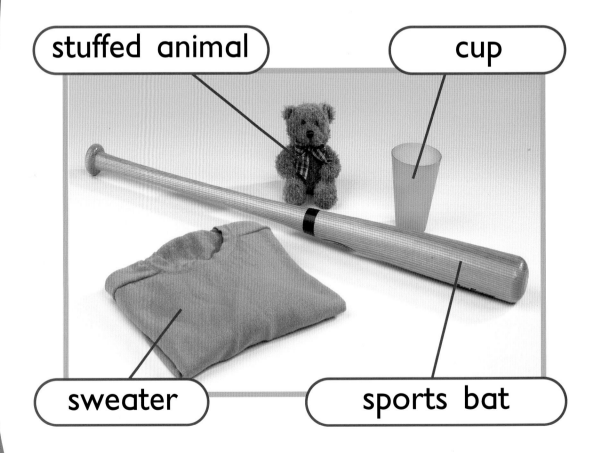

stuffed animal

cup

sweater

sports bat

Glossary

carved
cut

chemical preservative
stuff that keeps materials from damage

hose
tube that carries water from a faucet

material
stuff that something is made of

rigid
stiff and hard to bend

rough
bumpy and uneven

Index

batter 5
game 4
hard 16
heavy 10–11, 12, 13
hitting 5, 10
hose 19
light 11
material 7
pillow 17
pitcher 4
plastic 11, 12
rough 14
smooth 15
soft 17
splinter 14

Answers to the quiz on page 22

The bat and the cup are hard.

The stuffed animal and the sweater are soft.

Note to parents and teachers

Reading for information is an important part of a child's literacy development. Learning begins with a question about something. Help children think of themselves as investigators and researchers by encouraging their questions about the world around them. Each chapter in this book begins with a question. Read the question together. Look at the pictures. Talk about what you think the answer might be. Then read the text to find out if your predictions were correct. Think of other questions you could ask about the topic, and discuss where you might find the answers. Assist children in using the picture glossary and the index to practice new vocabulary and research skills.